MW01713593

"Dan Ames' *Feasting at the Table of the Damned* is rough and luscious, mean and sensuous. A book to be sipped neat, then rolled around the mouth like a fine single-barrel bourbon. It may even burn a little, but that's part of the pleasure."

~Michael Zadoorian, author of *The Leisure Seeker and The Lost Tiki Palaces of Detroit*

"Reading *Feasting at the Table of the Damned* is like taking a walk through a constant sunset with each step dipped in truth and wine . . . I remember being impressed and startled as a reader only a few times . . . reading *Catcher in the Rye* in my adolescence, reading Bukowski in my early twenties . . . well, I'm much older now and this collection strikes me much the same way, poetry with a pace and image that refuses to let me go.

~David LaBounty, author of *Affluenza*

Feasting at the Table of the Damned

poems by

Daniel Ames

AQUARIUS PRESS

Detroit, Michigan

Feasting at the Table of the Damned

Copyright © 2011 by Daniel Ames

All rights reserved. No part of this publication may be reproduced, stored in a retrieval system, or transmitted in any form, or by any means, electronic, mechanical, recording, photocopying or otherwise without the prior written permission of the publisher.

Cover Art: "El Jaleo" by John Singer Sargent, 1882
Cover Design: Bill Zalenski, THIELDesign, www.thiel.com

Living Detroit Series
Aquarius Press
www.aquariuspressbookseller.net

ISBN 978-0-9846212-6-2

Library of Congress Control Number 2011905072

Printed in the United States of America

for ROBERT GORDON AMES
1933-1996

Table of Contents

While I was musing the fire burned.
~Psalm 39:3

Bearings

they said, you're losing it
they said, you're blind
out of touch
lost in a world filled with art and noise

drowning in unkept promises
broken proclamations
sleepwalking in a night filled with songs
of the whiskey women

you will die young and unhappy
they predict
no, I counter
I'm just getting my bearings

Cheap and Damned

scattered shards of coveted soul
greenstick fractures left for dead
you stabbed the purloined truth
for a peephole dime

send the baby to the killing floor
hammer blows and shot shell breech
you ripped the flawless womb
for a twisted strand of liquid vice

shoot the innocent and burn the body
toss her lamb from the highest hill
shred some skin for a breathless gasp
at the table of the damned

Emancipation in Black

the half moon in the chaise lounge
whispered her song of the South
a vermilion whisper
heard only by the alligators and me
the music was cottony soft
Spanish moss tickled her flat brown stomach
an obscenely large bucket
poured its contents onto the grass
matted brown by nineteen fleeing turtles
a trickle of sweat
twinkled its lighthouse signal to me
along the small of her back
oh Poseidon you wrinkly old bastard
you will not deny me tonight
for I have seen the green and verdant bustle
of Charleston at dawn
I will trade my load of spice
for anything grown in your tropical triangle
you who half-raise an eyelid
to see if I'm looking at you
and sure as the Moravians
laboring hard in Old Salem
you will hear the call
of my two hundred and sixty eight organ pipes
humming in perfect, hot harmony

Like Valkyrie

we came like rage to the brain of the Earth
like a brazen horde of hellions
spewing fire and venom

we came like a blade forged in poison
dancing with flame
like a set of fangs poised
over the flesh of the lamb
dripping

granted, there were the sparrows and the larks
the gentle flight of minds
in harmony with the dream of light

twisting ribbons of silk
wrapped in the lips of a lover
who rode in with waves
from the bay
on crests of lavender

but no

the ones she wanted descended like Valkyrie
scorched and fuming
boiling mercury
dashed from the fist of God

and she bore them sixteen towering sons
who strode through the meadows of Euphoria

stomping the ochre blossoms
beneath their heavy leather boots
they were her chosen ones
they who knew nothing

but to slake their undying thirst
with nectar sucked from the defeat
of the innocents

Where The Train Runs Out of Track

beyond the Elysian Fields
in a swath of scrub oak and gravel
in the distance a small farmhouse
without windows or a door
a hawk flies overhead with a red tail
and an eye for what's beyond
this is where you and I now stand

the railroad ties soaked in creosote
black and fissured
the ghosts of tall weeds
are carried along by the wind
the silence presses on our temples
the heat smothers our skin
you and I and the glassy scent of gasoline

there may have been plans
to keep laying track
we can almost make out the linear banks
of earth ahead
a heat wave shimmers
beyond the broken landscape
where you and I try to see

you turn and look back
I was waiting for you to do it
I would have been disappointed if you hadn't
because then the years along the way

would have tendrils
viscous remnants of you and I

you turn back to the front
and as your gaze passes me
I wonder if you look at me
or if you continue to swivel
without interruption or contemplation
toward the precipice ahead
neither you nor I comprehend

at long last the faint smile comes
and I am thrilled and reassured
I take your hand and your calm acceptance
like a thousand times before
the hawk is gone and a young child
comes out of the farmhouse
she hears the train that is you and I

Soft Opening

before the inner sanctum goes out there
and becomes a sack of hay
propped up and spread wide
the perfect martyr
for all to unleash
the fury of their quivers

Before the pollen bursts from the pregnant seed
we will have a soft opening
quiet and private
soft breath and lilac perfume
for the ones we allow over the moat
and into the warm wetness
of our deepest hopes

Evening Magnolia

you cannot leave her alone
you cannot abandon her
leave her on the pier encased in morning fog
before the heat of the Carolina morning
swamps her

you cannot leave her
to face the razor teeth of dusk alone
she will grasp for a weapon
her fingers will encircle the air
of what you used to be

unsnake the life hanging over the tree limb
untie the knot forming the noose
and take your rightful spot beside her
until time and the scent of evening magnolia arrive

Gods Numbered

when they handed out gods
I was at the back of the line
unable to see what was happening up front
I figured by the time I got there
all the good ones would be gone
I had #672 and they were calling out #11
and with them closing the place at sundown
right when darkness arrived
there was no chance
I could see by then
they were handing out the shitty ones
days old
the gods that weren't even trying anymore
so I left and tossed my number to the ground
in the parking lot
scraping the bottom of the celestial barrel
a homeless guy picked it up and ran inside
shouting Hallelughia!

Perplexing When

maybe it was the afternoon
or perhaps it was first thing in the morning
when the day's hope sagged under the dry sun
or was it when you were closed to the day
and God's smile eased into a frown
or when the little one got bigger
maybe you'd seen it hours before
when the hummingbird drank from your soul
and flew on to another tree
or when the garden lay fallow
and the first of the weeds arrived
no not then
probably when you were stripped naked
your muscles peeled from your bones
nerves tied in knots
projected fate scrambled and burned
there's nothing like a slick piece of glass to show you the rapid
decline of flawed and troubled truth
maybe when the rib was plucked
from disintegrating hope
and the little wren skipped into shadow
maybe that was when you
stopped caring

this is all for Nancy

Montana

there is a place in Montana
windswept and cocoa colored
pearls and ribbons of pink
pour through canyons of flesh
long limbs taut and salty
tangy with a feminine musk
that lingers on my chin
like a cinnamon tinged memory

there is heaven in Montana
unbeknownst to everyone
a private arroyo filled with the fickle brush
whose juice is sweet
and where I lap with easy kindness
though the tangle is dense
with a thousand wild buffalo
I guide through the path

there is a place in Montana
where the sky bursts with heavy dew
and the curvaceous clouds
are punctuated with small pink sugars
that loll on my tongue
like a thousand Chinese masters
pulling on my hair
and pushing me so grinding and true

Montana has a place that is like a mouth
succulent and moist

a canyon draw history has left for me
to ravage with abandon
a winding river that leads to the mouth
of a perfect silk patch
where I will lay my head
but not rest until she has found peace

The Proving Rail

make the train talk, he said
you won't be a man if you can't make the train talk
squawking on that old guitar

the rail lines listened
and judged if the boy could make something
inanimate
speak

bring life, they said, like Jesus
give a soul to millions of pounds of steel
and steam

make the train talk

take a blank page
make it sing from the rafters
like a choir pushing the steamy air
further upward

to the chugging heavens

Roku

your fingers with chopsticks long and slender
green eyes resplendent with the Canadian tundra
a jawline as smooth and unbroken as a river of ice

sake for you sapporo for me sashimi for both
the wasabi fires through the troughs of longing
behind my eyes and out through my long days

yellowtail and scallion, salmon and ahi
soy sauce and ginger and a hot wet towel
sapporo for me, sake for you, sapporo for me

I am American you are Canadian
the night is Japanese
my past and yours meet
under a flowing silk robe
and I ask for your chopsticks
to taste something sweet

back in the room where Clinton or Reagan slept
I open the doors so the sound of the Pacific can roll in
along with the vaporous calls of money from Malibu

sapporo for me, sapporo for you, room service hastens
a steaming hot shower we recreate the start of Roku
I marvel at the crystalline beauty of a Canadian willow

wasabi pales in comparison to the fire from your skin
the way it burns my tongue

and scorches my brain
every inch of you
incites the fury of an American dream

sesame and wild
blue with the depths of salt and current
our friends from the East would laugh
at our hungry mouths
simply to spite them
we mix our metaphors
add Chinese

clouds and rain
clouds and rain
clouds and rain

Melting

from a distance it looked like yoga or meditation
facing the mountains of Santa Monica
the blue plate of the Pacific
on the soft green grass near Ocean
as the distance closed
and the bits of grass on her sweatpants
became noticeable
as the holes in her t-shirt appeared
the knots in her hair
the back and forth motion not
a rhythmic dance of relaxation
but the frayed ends of a brain burning
it wasn't a peaceful morning in Santa Monica
but a mound of flesh and bone being
eaten by the acid
of dying dreams

The Caress of Egg Shells

it is the rib cage of a sparrow
the spine of a hummingbird
the morning breath of a gypsy
clouded with eucalyptus
and the egg shell caress
of promising morning mist

there is no way to pursue,
she must come to you for you
and the quartersawn oak
surrenders noiselessly to the footsteps
of the exquisitely puritan soul
who surfaces beyond glass

she is a mirror right now
one side is pure reflection
the other side is of the not knowing or seeing
but one day will emerge
a two-way tunnel of glass

the wooden planks will sound one final time
the sparrow and the hummingbird will lift
there will be evening death, then, final blind flight

Afterthought

I am always the afterthought
the last blush of color
once the petal has hit the ground
I am the soft blur of motion
tickling the periphery of light
the detail devoid background
at best a utilitarian frame
my purpose to merely focus the eye
on the hero composition
I am the last car on the train
yet most likely
the first to arrive
at oblivion

Mahalo

join me in the river of red
as it gushes beneath the escarpment
below an outcropping black and apoplectic

the bubbles harden and shatter on the surface
sharp enough to shred a good pair of leather boots
but we swim in the heat, blissful and oblivious

we see other rivers, other diversions, yet stay on course
always, always, we are headed to the sea
where the cold water meets us with barbed teeth

it is a cascade of steam and slow movement
an eruption mistaken for smoke, instead, relief
a creation of structure is a possibility not provable

hold my hand during the metamorphosis
I will caress you amidst the transition to vapor
when the cold envelops us
and we say a warm goodbye

Convention Boulevard

there's a convention up ahead
once you've circumnavigated madness
everyone will be there who isn't someone

we'll toast our depositions to the judge
and drink shooters all midnight long
once you've transmigrated misery
bring your unrequited fantasies
and a dish of malfeasance to pass

we'll get a bus with a stripper pole
and drive around our blackhearts
all abysmal long

there's a convention up ahead
the life you could have lived
will be speaking after lunch

Over

was it over when the Germans
bombed Pearl Harbor?
was it over when Custer
slaughtered the Japanese?
meet me at the hot tub with your bottles of beer
and we'll toast the farces that make up
our mutually falsified history
meet me where Genghis Kahn
plundered the Hoover Dam
let's make love where Alexander the Great tortured the Incas
but missed Macchu Picchu

Bombs

they are stashed everywhere
placed with no master plan
quite haphazardly

no collective time frame
for final resolution

I can hear them like
a schizophrenic orchestra
at night when I can't sleep

tick tick tick tick tick tick tick tick tick
tick…tick…tick…tick…tick…tick…tick
tick………tick………tick………tick……….

perhaps one is in a cupboard
another beneath the foundation
probably one is concealed behind a half-truth
another slipped between the veils of exaggeration

the only consolation may be that while
this field of imminent destruction
is a composite of our lives
there is a certain security in knowing that each
little surprise package
found its quiet private home

via our own pale, gentle hands

Francesca

there have been transgressions along the border
even a tunnel or two were burrowed in the night

the division is long and rugged, miles of rock
cliffs and canyons rattlesnakes and scorpions

and it is not a straight line

vigilance is nearly impossible
twenty four hours a day
the nights are the worst
when shadows play with your mind

it is possible to go over
and come back unnoticed
but the other side changes you,
the language and the food

you are never the same

Pluff Mud

you come from the low country
with your cast net and crooked teeth
the wisteria is monstrous behind the tavern
you walk with a soft, sweet shamble
as the breeze delivers its salt and magnolia fruit
the liquor bites
with a particularly fanged venom
the way I sink my ivories
into the mocha flesh of your shoulders
with my tongue still warm from the grits
it sits out there, doesn't it?
between the sea and shore
hidden by sweet grass and strange canals
it can be harvested, brought up
cut into soft blocks and thrown
on a wheel by a fat man and an old stone
but you and I like it out there
deep, dark and rank
so we can smother each other with it
and listen to it suck

Sage

I don't care what you think of me
I don't think of me at all
except when I'm calling and drinking beer
when she's sprawled on the bed in impossibly tight jeans
and I'm thinking of the beauty of the sage flowers
underneath the thrusting moon

yeah I know how you see me
a disgusting menace that galls and frightens you
that grabs you by the throat and smashes you
against the bathroom wall

that reeks of penance misgiven
of nickels in the collection basket
of orange leaves dropping
to the Hawks Inn ground

yeah I know what you think of me
but do you know what I think of you
and your shiny little earrings
and manicured lawns
of you and your mouth
that swallowed the burst of convicts

I Don't Know Doug Parson

somewhere in Florida there's a place
you can rent jet skis
and parasail
and get drunk

he told me to say tell 'em Doug Parson sent you
he was the brother-in-law
snorkeled with the guys
who ran the jet skis

I said his name, the first guy didn't now him
the second guy said he knew a lot of Dougs
the third guy finally recognized the name
gave me a token discount

I' d like to try that with God
when he won't let me into heaven
for all the patently awful things I've done
and said and lied about

I'll tell him Doug Parson sent me
you remember Doug
he'll look at me with incomprehension
we'll see how that goes

Wounds

you roll up the cuff of your jeans
expose a smooth brown skin
see this? you say
that's from when you hurt me
years ago

ah, that's nothing, I say
I pull the worn collar away from my neck
and point at my pale throat
that's from when you lied to me
way back when

we do a couple more rounds of this
as the cabin light sways above us
rendering no judgment
the wood floor creaks
finally calling it a draw

we knock our paper cups together
and drink the cheap whiskey
then we climb up the stairs
fire up the engines
and head back out to sea

The Murdered Years

they are strewn from here to Tijuana
tossed into the dumpster
thrown from the overpass
buried in the field of unknowing

their last moments were not pleasant
rich with strife and frothing
crushed by the hoary thumb of
corporate America

kicked from the car during marital strife
passed out beneath the bar stool
while a friend rifles pockets for cash
and the bartender looks the other way

no detective has taken up the cold case
no pictures have been placed on milk cartons
they are gone and forgotten
unmarked graves
wandering eternity

the slaughter has slowed a bit
but the blood thirst is not fully slaked
a year goes for a walk and never returns
a year picked up a john, didn't come back

they are the kind of moments no one cares about
no relatives will put pressure on the authorities

the days, weeks, months will remain missing
and no one is holding out hope they're still alive

so we go on

we put one foot in front of the other
we scratch at the foot that is no longer there
a song catches our ear and we turn
until the memory vanishes

one day, maybe, the cadaver dogs will howl with glee
the coroner will dissect where it all went wrong
someone will mourn the murdered years
say what a waste, they were so young and innocent

Boots

she said, when I wear these boots no one fucks with me
when I tie my past like a scarf around my throat
I can freeze the blood
of every naive and unabashed up-and-comer
when I slide on my desire like glowing black stockings
I can make the uninitiated beg
for the feel of raw and stinging wood
and when I slip my angry black leather belt
from its rusty hook
the ambitious and guileless cower
like a thousand condemned souls
when I close my fist, my rings golden
with a youth well spent
the warriors of Gilead surrender
with a breathless whimper
and when my shoulders
feel the rough comfort of my serape woven with the fibers
of a fierce and relentless vengeance
you will soon realize
these are not my clothes after all, she says,
they are warning signs

A Spoiled Walk

spoiled the walk in the woods
not knowing the names of anything
what is that plant or flower or tree,
who the hell knows, it's green

what is that insect, that bird,
that type of sloping hill cut at the bottom
that rock worn on both sides
with fossils crammed in the middle

so familiar to the feeling
of not knowing why she says what she says
why the love is always flowing out
like a tide toward the sound

not understanding why he acts like an animal
alone in the penthouse
why the pearls inlaid in the sidewalks
on Fifth Avenue twinkle for so few

why there is such a thing as a human
who can steal other humans
and hide them in a twisting corridor
littered with butchered lives

such a spectacular failure
unable to recognize the breed of woman
who thunders through my daily dreams
with sweaty glistening buttocks

a veritable argyle
shining with slick dark pools of forgetfulness
no surprise I am not cognizant
of the butterflies soaring in circles above me

perhaps some research is in order,
meet with John Muir and Sigmund Freud
a little Carl Jung and W.H. Audubon
we could sort it out together

but I have a feeling I am so deep into this thing,
these woods without end
besides, that meeting was never really going to happen

I would have missed it
still hiking through swamp muck and poison oak
picking the bugs from my eyes
and bloody ticks from my aching thighs

grasping for the name of the woman
whose footfalls shatter my nightly sleep
and leaves me marveling at the complexities
of nature's web of evolution

and how there is so much to know
and to understand and it is hopeless
a dizzying maze of names in Latin,
urges and motivations and sexual deviations

an entire canon of flora and fauna
twisted laws of attraction
that gush through the soil and create curves
that are called something

Twisted Salvation

I like the twisted type of salvation
where sin and redemption weave
a thick rope tossed over burning beams
singe morning's teary-eyed regret

I appreciate the beauty of dogged prayer
with the stench of last night's smoke
still fresh in my nostrils and the stains
of midnight gorging glowing on my lips

the leap is brief and thrilling
the fall with smashed shoulder blades
and lungs shot forth with heavy breath
stunning as the weight of bedrock

every time I reach for her the awareness
hits me like a hand raised to strike
the eyes like handholds, clinging
and then we're on our way down

The Bitch Tree

I love to lounge beneath the bitch tree
wrap my arms around her hostile trunk
feel the scratching of harsh, brittle leaves

the bitch tree provides shade with attitude
love with constant reproach
fruit simultaneously sweet and bitter

oh for a forest of bitch trees
an unbroken stand of beauty and anger
a floor of fallen curses

lumbermen be warned
your chains and axes will not harm
my beloved bitch

in the land of myself
the state tree is the bitch
and she is protected

Acceptance

it warms the soul, the opposite of no
causes the sun to burn the cloud
and fill the field with light

when the door opens,
you burst with speed toward it
not noticing the welcome mat

and how worn it is

The Glory of Greece

the Aegean Sea beckons
with its medallions of gold
vessels from the sand of Tunis
carry shrunken heads
the junks of Asia
boom with the bursting of spice
and a thousand slaves
die on barren Egyptian rock

lust is so Mediterranean
even floating off the coast of Jamaica
thousands of tiny little islands
signaling from the bottom of the sea
seared by the Arabs and stolen from the Greeks
we are headed toward Gibraltar
shuddering with our load

I am preparing for our bed
by layering myself in garlic
while you anoint yourself
with delicate ambrosia
our legs will entwine,
tendons rippling like a Michelangelo
and the halls of the Vatican
will bleed with our sins

Refills from the Pharmacy

I have a great dresser
a John Widdicomb with two sections
I use the top mostly
it is filled with all of my various medications
that work together
to help me get through the day
I've got the usual battery
of vitamins and Tylenol
and baby aspirin to thin the blood
leftover painkillers
from the summer when a piece of steel
shot out from underneath the lawnmower
and buried itself in the bone of my foot
right at the front are bigger bottles
that include shame, hopeless resignation,
thinly concealed fury
bright, sun-drenched manifestations
of insecurity (I must have gotten that one from Costco –
the bottle is huge)
a dark brown bottle filled with poison supplied by family
and rivals
the bedroom starts to fill with the light of dawn
and I start twisting off caps,
emptying contents into
my white, shaky, outstretched palm
I wonder how many I can swallow at once

Four Songs

there are four major songs in my canon,
my first tunes sitting around me
in steel folding chairs like a support group

the first song talks about our horrible night together how I
barged into the first measures like a drunken billy goat
and produced some discordant howlings
it wasn't really a song but more a clearing of the throat

the second song went much like the first with a few drums some
light percussion and then at least a rhythm and halfway decent
vocals but the echo afterward was painful and hollow
an empty dance floor

I made a real leap in maturity on my third song
a lot of tempo changes
a very seasoned band that played from a balcony
overlooking a small city
along with an especially strong flute section

outside the room, where we are sitting, there are some auditions
knocking on the door, they don't belong here really, just odd
riffs and drum runs that never actually caught on to any sort of
real tune

when the fourth song finally starts playing from the stereo back
by the coffee maker, everyone listens because it is a group of
notes held together by experience and professionalism and no
small amount of psychosis

there really is very little for me to say—yes, I created
this playlist, and I was a shitty conductor, but the seats in each
section were taken on a purely volunteer basis

I never promised anyone I could actually play

Closer

a thousand empty spaces in the parking lot
and you choose the one next to me
a hundred empty chairs on the patio
and you sit on my left
a dozen empty lockers at the club
and you pick 27 so we can bump elbows

a billion pure oxygen molecules
and you just have to pollute the ones near me
with your stale breath and tired soul

no matter where I am
no matter how hard I've worked
to put an amenable amount of space between you and I
you figure out a way to come closer
you are brazen

this space is pure gold to me
a layer of diamonds
a river of platinum
a buffer made of rare jade

and yet you rob me every day
every chance you get
you scoop the diamonds
from their black velvet perches
into your cheap burglar's bag
you piss into my platinum river

and drop my jade
shattering it into thousands of cheap little trinkets

you smile at me and talk non stop
never realizing that I desperately want to report you
to the gods of space worshippers
who understand the supreme violations
you have committed
and of which you are a chronic offender

give me the one gift
for which I will cherish you forever…

distance

The Dogs of Disillusion

what do you want
packing your arteries full of shit
gray skin crawling at the sight of dawn
chipped teeth gnashed in fury over flakes of inconsequence

the Hispanic maids don't want to fuck you
the hot tub is full of angry memories
and herpes

recalcitrant and homeless
your dreams are tossed into the dumpster
behind the hotel
by the garbage trucks

a mother and her daughters
45, 17 and 14
were by the pool
hard medium and soft

there's no future in the screams
of wasted times

why don't you ball up your sweaty little fists
and swat them
at the dogs of disillusion

Blues Face

I grind my fingers against the strings
trying to smear the notes
choking the slides the hammer-ons and the bends
my left hand is made of iron
my right hand is a blur
until the pick snaps
I play hard and fast and furious
my instrument is in danger of breaking
like a piece of driftwood over the knee
and I wonder why the music
sounds so forced

In The Shallows

I live in the shallows where the blue rocks wait
where the studded sand listens
ankle deep at best

an uninteresting border
a loose rope around
life in the depths

I live in the shallows where sound doesn't carry
thermal layers insulate
keep the joy from spreading

nothing takes root here
burned by the pale sun
trampled by flip flops

there just isn't much
to work with here
no substance

things like people
skid along the surface
until they land, gone

far from the shallows

Epilogue of Flames

I predict my finish will possess
an untoward and mighty flourish
a flurry of three thousand songbird wings
among sensuous vapors of glee
an orgy of peach and lavender angels
flesh rosy with desire
plump fuchsia lips
glistening with death's sugary dew

clasped in the iron fist of the dead it will remain
an ivory hollowed talisman of the life shallowly led
an unexpected burst from an extinguished rose
cloaked in the dirt of yesterday's uprooting
the guilts and half-formed wishes
whose gathered whispers combine
to create a most unremarkable man

framed against the greatness of a star littered light
so coarse and cornfed like every tooth gritted dream
the regal and blueblooded ghosts judge from above
and piss on the peons whose hopes are barren

how dare you strive for an epilogue of flames?
a dessert of custardy excess, feast of the flesh
it simply is not done the book of heroes insists
do not rise they decree, you may only return

The Truth

you can move mountains with those grinning smirking
shadows
you can conquer entire island countries with an effortless
underhand
these are the basics for someone like you
merely the ground floors of a grand edifice
you'll have finished by fall
but that one true thing, that one beautifully lofted spiral
spinning in the purity of an honest man's heart
that is the moment when the smile slides
from your tanned and polished façade
and crashes to the echo
legs and arms and spindles
pinwheeling

Fragile Magic

you float on the raft
lashed together with pyrite strands
of forgotten mornings

when we ran together
springs and fingers and auburn shimmer
spirits hovering over an apricot mouth
you were the beginning the middle and the end
the disconcerted vapor of an ancient fragile magic

a mesh of muscular bodies stitched into the void
left by those who came before

but there was no one

it surged from dawn a melodic dance
performed between two alabaster souls
hungry for nothing
tasting the rise

it falls through the tumbling stars of time
a splintering spray of shrapnel and rhyme

you can see the orbiting ruins

The Fishing Tree

dead but tall with synapses long and crooked
they sat
azure desiccated talon strong
the first year virginal and green it was crowded
shoulder to shoulder we stood vigilant
the river churned wafts of insect riddled dreams
one by one they disappeared
the ancient reptile slipped
into the depths of oblivion
while we swallowed the sulfur
alone and empty the hunters fled
for the great maternal winds of fear
I toasted their persecution
and cried for their bones

Partridge Road

it sings a drink among the fallen leaves
slants the light from the sun's storied fall
slides along the grass behind her smile
rides in rhythm to the shallow bark of fear
I know I've heard it when the ghosts stand down

it was the purity denied that curdled your shame
the walk from hope into roiling disdain
it was a parlor heist unveiled from afar
the newborn seethed at the ancient's grin
I know I've seen it when the ghosts stand down

it drips a sap sugary and stale
rains a protest to your withering back
those aren't echoes fresh notes being rung
thorns slash the perfect sheen still very young
I know I've felt it when the ghosts stand down

Ties

she clung like dust to the ring of the asteroid belt
windblown and roasted by the helium flares

a passenger running from the fall of burning
riding the echo of death's black and copper bell

the shadowy glint on the raven's dripping beak
a frothy breath from the dying river's past

you chose wrong and shared the wine of sorrow
cursed the buds of spring in someone else's yard

Key Deer

he climbed the porcine edge
beneath her blue eyes
stabbed by palmettos his hand thrust
into her jagged teeth
she said that's not what I'm about

the flowers rose from earthen springs
dewy with masks of gold
diamonds blazed in his palms
he ground silver in his teeth
for the key deer born along the Estero River
she said that's not what this is about

he rose then a rod to spare a staff to throw
slippery with aspiring lips and sugary grain
the lemons sweat and glisten
shaded by the lanai

she said that's not what we're about
he knelt
fire around him they shouted into his ears

purple shaded his face
he said
you don't know
either

Romeo

at the back of the barn
we met the girl from Romeo
hair limp and straight
and vaguely blonde

skin very white and bold
aggressive even
we wish we could remember more
but the cows were balling

the roof of the barn lifted off
and we were faced with moonlight
a shadowy and slippery figure
dashing in and out

it's tough to be
one of the harder customers
in a farm full of chickens
and neutered lambs

fill the slop troughs
with your sloppy oats
and messy mysteries
just solve the damn thing

but it isn't going to happen
because you've got the thoughts
of an angel ascending
and a demon shrinking from the truth

crawl back into your minivan
and drive the long narrows
with a jaw that's clenched
but pure and uninfected

your thoughts of the barn
however are like the Amish
driving along in their buggies
simple and unsoiled

Trade

you can lie to the gods who make your baskets
woven with sweet grass
you can listen to your footsteps
on the wide ancient pine boards
but I can hear the screams coming
from Bunce Island
where the gray hairs are plucked to fool the buyer
let's sit in our mansion south of broad street
and haggle over the women too young to fuck
you inhale the sweetly succulent flesh of the tobacco
crushed by feet unnaturally white
let's send a cannonball toward the wide open harbor
and let them know
we mean business

Of the Taiga

she emerges from the earth's dark orifice
bawling with hunger
and a rage fully blackened with cold
she emerges as if loaded
with the gentle push of a thumb
black powder and yellow fangs gnashing

the search is on for the hundred heads
left to mark the trail
a pyramid of lost thinkers
piled high by a methodical death

there is no time for what is not,
this is the time for what is
and as she thunders down the speckled trail
she spies the entrance
marked with a thousand heads

a pile of poseurs devoured and shat out
by that giant thing
called truth

Life Poorly Done

leave her there in the honeysuckle vines
chagrined and jilted compared to them
those are cats eyes alone and bright
fearful and fierce silent and sad
a wandering minstrel among the dying
a bamboo shoot shred by a single claw
a darkroom image in the rearview mirror
she didn't bother to wave goodbye
the pit in her stomach dissolved years ago
the early evening moon lights her face
shadows conceal the path that led you here
can you hear the people in the room above her
why did they get to live and not you
congratulate yourself on a life poorly done
should have switched the signs like the Germans
sent her off into the meadows at Giverny
painted nude in the gauzy light of Monet's garden
she gave you everything she had
you gave her this
an epilogue twenty chapters long
a decade of dust on the dining room wall
a phone that rarely rings save for
reverb from the hospital

Lipo

I went for liposuction today
but I told the guy to only take out
the stuff that makes snotty comments to my wife

and the part that has no patience
when the kids are arguing about hair ties
and get that big glop of resentment
hiding near my spleen
created by the blunt refusal of Miss Meriweather
to welcome my advances

take out the stuff that keeps tossing up marshmallows
onto the blank page and loves clichés
and questions whatever it is I'm doing
like it's the kind of thing worthy of interpretation

best of all, put it in a big giant jar
and I'll take it back to work, put it on a platter
and make a ring of gourmet crackers
with a sign that says
"help yourself"

Captain Nasty

the smile on the street
the lips that part
to reveal
freshly brushed teeth
are buried by sunset
in the dark flesh
of sin and sweat
a feast of young
and unknowing flesh
hidden from the neighbors
by soft folds
of Roman shades
and heavy lidded looks
of private engorgement

Darla

I once feasted on the soul of my neighbor
laughed as the rabbit's spine was cracked
tossed the hair of the brunette
who I loved

but you didn't see me did you
no one saw me
I was the enigma at the back of the room
but enough about me
let's talk about you

jonas
you traitor
with your tiller
in the back

grinding and digging
and collecting
your gelatinous secrets

Pico

there's liquid gold inside that glass
it calls me from above
seeks to listen and understand
while the women in my life
can only wonder
shit that's a laugh
says the migrant worker from Mexico
I had a wife and sister
they are whores and you don't even know
catch some shit feel the scabs dig in
and then you can laugh and write and die
while the lovely madrigal sings
on Pico

Death by Chimney

a fierce electric current something mechanical
inhuman above the fireplace
they said to go out at night look at the chimney
a cloud of bats frenzied whipping
like lines over a trout stream

the first person talked of a trapdoor,
regulations and breeding seasons
the second guy
a true Detroit 313 area code
said no problem
he was a wrinkled old black guy
probably eighty years old
got a Free Press? he said

he used two ladders to get to the top
fired up his Bic and got the job done
like all of the infiltrations and bad marriages
and hatred pure and poisoned

we can choose how we solve them
the clean, hard way or the fast, dirty way
I prefer solutions that start with a 313 area code

Truculence

she whispers into my truculence
and I succumb to that thing called faith
that blind old hag who left her brothers and sisters
under the overpass

she strokes her way into my soul
a divining rod slips from the heavens
a greasy old senior citizen
with stale coffee breath
and a proverb for any situation

she recounts the transgressions from a lifetime ago
with a glassine vision
the images move in a circular sway,
dashing from light to dark
truisms to falsehoods

this is a woman, my friend,
with whom you can ride the river
and gaze at the mountain

this is a woman
with a heart fired by the very furnace of Hell
yet beats with the sonnets of God

Early to Death

I have arrived early for my death
my planned departure was much later
but some things fell through

for instance, first thing this morning
I had planned to fall in love
but by the time breakfast was over,
I knew it wasn't going to happen

with certainty I had assumed later today
a gaggle of friends would come over
we would laugh about what young fools we were
somehow, though, they never showed

I was also convinced family matters would
occupy most of my afternoon
but I have fallen out of touch with them
accusations and injustices levied
but never forgotten

so I have arrived here early and taken my seat
wishing that I could have found something
else to do, somewhere else to go, someone
else to spend time with, to laugh and love

the magazines here suck, they are old and
uninteresting

at last, a door opens and I stand,
knowing it is my turn

but wishing that I was anywhere but here

wishing I was back at the point in my life
when I could have changed things
made it so that when this door opened
I wouldn't be here

wishing instead that I would be
very, very

late

A Splash of Mahogany

blame the penniless soldier for his incursions
into the cupboards of wheat
grind the bones of the neatly destroyed
stir them into your gin

hold up the mirror
to distort the sunflower's undeniable truth
and then you wonder
why they spiral with carbide tips
toward your skull
you're not stupid
just weak

a cracked sheet of mahogany splits
under the force of the wind
you will not be remembered
but the flames of cruelty
are eternal

The Others

there are other lives being led
unbeknownst to the close ones
there are phantoms being touched and caressed
in the haunted hotel rooms
near the freeway

the other lives keep mostly to the shadows
but occasionally burst onto the maple dance floor
and howl at the Swarovski crystal chandeliers
grinding their hips with the passion
only darkness can produce

they skitter along the recesses
of mottled skin and bone
when a door is thrown open
they run for the basement
where the bad people are
and where bad things are done
there are entire communities built
of lives strange to their hosts
they cuddle under trundle beds
have comforters made of shame
when the sun is out and green leaves feast

they are multiplying

Last Waltz

close but not touching they dance
not together
from memory without thought
the steps don't lead in the same direction

iron galvanized by magnetic waves
repel push back twist
the buffer zone

wrapped in wind and swirled with light
spinning careening occasionally they bump
they stiffen muscles tighten lips purse

I wonder how long we can do this

Flambeau

it was named after a river
warm youth caressed and rushed silly
under coffee stars
her cousin wheeled us through waves of heat
her lips were like sour mash and sweet
her nipple on my finger cupped breast to mouth
breath hot and soft and stale beer tinged
white cotton with fancy sleeves snug jeans
she lived out there where cousins dated cousins
but the night was pure if forgettable
a pair of cheap baubles
in a car under moving streetlights
that laughed as we made our turns passing

The Rogue

we walk the fields
the past crumbling under our tennis shoes
dreams burning brown
the shoulders of our dispirited gaze
each take a row and walk
make the hoe arc blaze in the light
stalwart and thick with veins
sever the rogue

walk a quarter mile
turn in a sweep
the weed twice as tall and twice as green
cut it off at the root with one savage blow
twelve hours a day blue pouring gray
kill the rogue

swallow the day at the bar in Waunakee
ride the sunset on your motorcycle shitfaced
in the titanium rain a twister on the hill

thinking of the girl with the vanilla breasts
and sheared shorts a sliver of egg ass
against succulent salty thighs
the way she held a cigarette between her fingers
she was low but juicy and interested
nail the rogue

flop on the futon bed in your one room
booze reek coming off you in great circular rings

stagger down the hallway to the Russian girl's room
her mother was a Cossack you are a farmer
cutting down the rogue

Alter

you can buy a house in Detroit
for five hundred dollars
stripped of everything
copper furnaces wiring fixtures
buy an entire block for a couple grand
your own domain of hollow shells
gutted for scraps

be the mayor of a ghost town
president of a memory
emperor of an echo

the wind whistles through vacant eyes
grass grows through faulty floors

I've met a few houses like that
and a few of those landlords

the structure is there

nothing inside

Guys with Rollerbags

in a line straight out of the bonfire café
blue shirts with stripes
one following the other
off to their gate
and their plane
away but not free

that rollerbag
right behind you
riding your ass
like an angry tailgater

insistent

not willing to be left behind

Erosion

river water cuts through rock
winds back upon itself
recognizes the insanity of its behavior
reflects upon layers of earth
its silly journeys revealed

you and I are like those currents
charge retreat charge retreat
refuse to admit that every turn taken
was the wrong one

Toad

there are a lot of questions
I don't have the corresponding answers
I don't know who does
I don't care who does
the answers don't interest me
because the questions don't interest me
the questions are like black carbon pits
belching from the smokestack
of a woman
with a mind cut and beveled
like azure Egyptian crystal
and as dull as the skin of a toad

Peppers

the squirrels don't eat them because
underripe peppers are much hotter
mild only at the end of the growing season

occasionally, you'll see one with little bite marks
where an inexperienced scavenger thought
he'd hit the jackpot

you've got marks like those
where someone thought they could
take a bite

but when their mouths caught fire
they understood
they weren't ready for you

Daughter

a carapace of pure delicacy
a shade of fragile gold
a movement both sound and unbroken
timed to exquisite perfection
a drink of crystal
that ripples with the touch of surrender
she is the glow of a memory
the hope of a heart
shuddering with deep, heavy breaths

Scorched Earth

I purchased a scorched earth policy
from my insurance agent
it covers everything
past present future
wife marriage kids
house job debt

you just sign on the dotted line
then list your items
booze, distance, vultures and lies

it's good for the rest of your life
or early death
or misery
whatever comes first

but they will come
eventually
to collect

A Face Disfigured

I wonder what it looked like
how I felt before
the shattered nights
weeping streets
sucker punches

it is my face
and it isn't
it is theirs, too
they who watched
unrepentant

the visions that sliced
like dull knives
the heat that burrowed cheeks

it is a face
I try not to look at

Him

what is he doing here?
his head is monstrous
a blood splatter
among the renaissance masterpieces

he is nothing but a boweevil
among the softest and most pure cotton

a necessary evil
says the lark
in the serviceberry

Room To Swing

there is a stillness among men
a vacuum
room for violence

if necessary fill it with noise
artificial laughter
discussions instantly forgotten

but I'm always thinking of the violence
waiting for its arrival
with giddy anticipation

Coarse

my mistress is coarse
a burlap whore
rough around the knuckles
when she blinks
steel wool rakes furrows along her eyeballs
her breath sends rivulets of liquefied skin
dripping

she is my lover
and who can withstand
love's allure
whispering through her
siren of
agony

Made

along the planks of despair
I wept
over the arc of the sun
its mission accomplished at last
long last
the sea grass was tipped with dew
my fledgling osprey
held the shafts of delicate gold
in her mullioned wings
triumphant

The Pheasant of Detroit

the empty spaces of Detroit
remind me of our own scorched pasts
where burned out buildings stand
sagging like painful memories

neighborhoods and grand structures
created in a hurricane of hubris
now looked back on with shame
and the guilt over our rapid exit

in abandoned lots all over the city
the pheasant population is flourishing
in urban fields choked with tall grass
they escape the gaze of gangbangers

these birds are royalty
regal in their cloaks of despair
reminders that even surrounded
by the destruction of our past selves
something good can survive
and stand out

tiny explosions of color
a burgeoning colony
of pageantry
and spirit

Acknowledgments

I would like to thank Heather Buchanan for making this book possible, and Dr. Randall Horton for his editorial guidance. For their generosity, support and friendship, I give heartfelt thanks to: Michael Zadoorian, David LaBounty, John Jeffire, Ken Meisel, Lori A. May, Cassandra Sullivan, Lisa Greenwood-Hoffman, Lisa Pietsch, Becky Lincks Meyer, Brenda Moore Fritz, Amy Montoya, David Downing, Caitlin Constantine, and Jimmy Callaway.

Special consideration should be given to Annabel and Benedetta for their kindness, intelligence and humor.

I believe the most powerful truths tend to be the simplest. Like the notion you never really know what you are capable of until someone believes in you. Thank you, Susan, for everything.

~Daniel Ames
Grosse Pointe Park, Michigan
April 2011